A Closer Walk with God

Obeying God's Call to Ministry

Great Awakening book Series

Bishop Harriet S Anderson

Copyright

Book editing and formatting by: Dr Jacqueline Samuels

https://tinyurl.com/AuthorJNSamuels

Cover Design by Serve and Thrive:

https://serve-and-thrive-academy.thinkific.com/

Let's connect:
https://www.abundanceministries.co.uk/

IG: https://www.instagram.com/harrietanderson1045/

For other books by the author visit:

https://www.amazon.co.uk/Bishop-Harriet-S-Anderson/e/B0BLP8TQGB/

ISBN: 9798365860650

Contents

Dedication

I dedicate this book to the Holy Spirit who has faithfully walked with me throughout my life and ministry calling.

This book is also dedicated to my husband Pastor Simon Anderson who throughout my ministry has believed God with me and patiently stood by my side.

Acknowledgement

This book contains the truth the Holy Spirit brought my way as the Lord promised. I rest in faith that *"God looks over His Word to perform it."*

I give credit to the Godhead, my pastors prophets Robert and Jessica Kayanja and all the ministers who have been instrumental in my life and ministry. Thank you both for prayerfully nurturing me and always looking out for me.

The Late Colin Urqhart and the team of the Kingdom Faith Bible College: Thank you for training me on how to hear clearly from God.

I wish to acknowledge our Abundance Ministries brethren who continue to walk with us. You keep our fire burning as we joyfully serve God.

Special thanks go to Power of The Word Ministries family who continually nurture my spiritual growth and open their platform allowing me to share the love of Christ with them. God will reward your love and faithfulness in due season.

To my book editor, coach and friend, Dr Jacqueline Samuels: May the LORD reward your spirit of excellence and grant you continued favour as you serve His children in the Kingdom.

Introduction

I have been through it all. At a young age I was mentored by servants of God who taught me how to pray the Scriptures.

This book walks through the Great Awakening which began when I became a born-again believer. When we started to pray as young believers; we suddenly erupted into speaking in strange tongues, the heavenly language.

It is my prayer that you will be inspired to respond to the Holy Spirit's Voice as He guides you into your divine calling and purpose in this new season of your life.

We are embarking on an amazing transformational journey through these pages. Some of the amazing life lessons were learned through the hardest challenges I have faced. I am grateful for the unfailing and ever-present grace and mercy of God that have upheld and nurtured me throughout.

 Much work remains to be done in reaching the lost for Christ especially in these last days when God is pouring out His Spirit upon all flesh.

May God answer you in your moment of need and grant you the grace to endure for He remains faithful to supply all your needs from His glorious riches in Christ Jesus.

Let us prayerfully join our hearts and voices as we read David's earnest appeal for guidance and deliverance on the following page.

Psalm 143

1 Hear my prayer, O Lord, give ear to my supplications! in Your faithfulness answer me, and in Your righteousness.

2 Do not enter into judgment with Your servant, for in Your sight no one living is righteous.

3 For the enemy has persecuted my soul; he has crushed my life to the ground; he has made me dwell in darkness, like those who have long been dead.

4 Therefore my spirit is overwhelmed within me; my heart within me is distressed.

5 I remember the days of old; I meditate on all Your works; I muse on the work of Your hands.

6 I spread out my hands to You; my soul longs for You like a thirsty land. Selah

7 Answer me speedily, O Lord; my spirit fails! Do not hide Your face from me, lest I be like those who go down into the pit.

8 Cause me to hear Your lovingkindness in the morning, for in You do I trust; cause me to know the way in which I should walk, for I lift up my soul to You.

9 Deliver me, O Lord, from my enemies; in You I take shelter.

10 Teach me to do Your will, for You are my God; Your Spirit is good. Lead me in the land of uprightness.

11 Revive me, O Lord, for Your name's sake! For Your righteousness' sake bring my soul out of trouble.

12 In Your mercy cut off my enemies, and destroy all those who afflict my soul; for I am Your servant.

Chapter One: **Answering God's Call**

God has called you and made you His own. This emphasizes the uniqueness of each person and the fact that the gift imposes responsibility most especially. There are four things God is calling every believer and minister to do.

First, acknowledge God as the Father, Son and Holy Spirit (Creator, Redeemer, and Healer). This is focused on baptism playing an appropriate part within the body of Christ.

Second, the modern initiation role also contains a prayer of commission. If you are baptised in the Holy Spirit, you are called to worship and serve God.

Third, He is calling us to pray and believe in His Word and have faith in Him. God is also calling us into intercession to carry the burden for others.

Matthew 3:10 says,

> *"And even now the ax is laid to the root of the trees. Therefore every tree which does not bear good fruit is cut down and thrown into the fire."*

Forth, God is calling us to a selfless life, as revealed in 2 Corinthians 8:3-7,

For I bear witness that according to their ability, yes, and beyond their ability, they were freely willing, imploring us with much urgency that we would receive the gift and the fellowship of the ministering to the saints. And not only as we had hoped, but they first gave themselves to the Lord, and then to us by the will of God. So we urged Titus, that as he had begun, so he would also complete this grace in you as well. But as you abound in everything—in faith, in speech, in knowledge, in all diligence, and in your love for us—see that you abound in this grace also.

Have you fully committed to follow God's purpose and prompting? If not, now is the perfect time to purpose to follow Christ wholeheartedly. Respond aloud to the following statements:

1. **Will you persevere in resisting evil whenever you fall into sin? Will you repent and return to the Lord, with God's help?**

Your response: *Yes, I will.*

2. **Will you proclaim by word and example the Good News of God in Christ Jesus with the help of the Holy Spirit?**

Response: *Yes, I will.*

3. **Will you acknowledge Christ's authority over human society by prayer for the world and its leaders, defending the weak and seeking peace and justice?**

Response: *By God's help, yes, I will.*

4. ***May Christ dwell in your heart through faith that you may be rooted and grounded in love and bring forth the fruit of the Holy Spirit, Amen.***

All church members are called to participate in its apostolic mission (1 Peter 2:5), and the Holy Spirit gives various gifts and ministries through baptism.

Every member within the Body of Christ is called to offer their being as a living sacrifice and to intercede for the church and the salvation of the world. This is the corporate priesthood of all the children of God and the calling to serve as a minister of the Word of Life.

Luke 4:18 clarifies our part in the divine mission calling and purpose:

> *"The Spirit of the Lord is upon Me, because He has anointed Me to preach the gospel to the poor; He has sent Me to heal the brokenhearted, to proclaim liberty to the captives and recovery of sight to the blind, to set at liberty those who are oppressed..."*

God is bringing us to the place where we will know without any doubt that the Spirit of the Lord is upon us. Jesus promised to bring us a Comforter who will live with us and abide with us forever. This promise is revealed in John 14:16-26.

Verses 16-18 declares:

"And I will pray the Father, and He will give you another Helper, that He may abide with you forever— the Spirit of truth, whom the world cannot receive, because it neither sees Him nor knows Him; but you know Him, for He dwells with you and will be in you. I will not leave you orphans; I will come to you."

Jesus further goes on to emphasise in verses 23-24,

Jesus answered and said to him, "If anyone loves Me, he will keep My word; and My Father will love him, and We will come to him and make Our home with him. He who does not love Me does not keep My words; and the word which you hear is not Mine but the Father's who sent Me.

Knowing that we would need His assurance of peace, Jesus gave us this special gift (verses 25-26):

"These things I have spoken to you while being present with you. But the Helper, the Holy Spirit, whom the Father will send in My name, He will teach you all things, and bring to your remembrance all things that I said to you.

The Holy Spirit will abide with us in our daily routine of work and ministry. His presence can be manifested within every area of our daily lives including our homes, ministries, workplaces, politics, gymnastics, in social contexts and more.

Within the government: The Holy Spirit wants to be involved in local or national politics, campaigning, as well as areas that involve justice and peace.

Within the community: Ministry can involve taking part in street life and in our neighbourhoods. His presence should be revealed when we set up community projects.

In family settings: Ministry involves creating time for building family relationships.

Serving in church: Ministry involves representing the church on local projects and charities, while cooperating with other members.

In pastoral care: ministry involves visiting the sick, the burdened or house bound, in addition to organising a good neighbourhood scheme.

Chapter Two: **Call to Ministry**

In 1992 I was awarded a scholarship to study abroad and learn about understanding the Voice of the Holy Spirit. A kind lady called Althea Parsons invited me to the United Kingdom to join the Horsham Kingdom Faith Bible College. Althea raised funds with her family and friends to pay for my ticket to the UK.

When the Holy Spirit spoke to me to go to seven nations within Africa, I had to obey. The first country I visited was Kenya.

I shared the Gospel in the Kibera and Kariobang'i slums of Nairobi, Kenya and 500 people gave their lives to Christ. Many young people from the streets flocked to receive Christ. Glory to God! We went on the mission with Rev. Shin, a missionary from South Korea and missionary Jong.

Every time I obey the Voice of God, He opens a door for me and surprises me with material gifts I cannot afford in my own strength. In every nation I have visited, the key of obedience has unlocked the door.

On a mission at the Miracle Centre Church in Kampala, Uganda I met Pastor John Eckhart who walks in the prophetic. Shortly after Pastor Eckhart prophesied over my life the LORD opened new doors for me to minister around the world. Several unexpected events unfolded which taught me to fully trust the LORD in every detail in my life.

Praying for South Africa

I went to South Africa in 1994 where we prayed before Nelson Mandela was elected unopposed to become the first Black President of the South African Republic.

This was a pivotal time when Apartheid rulership was rife in South Africa and Black leaders had not been given any room to display their leadership qualities in the country.

Nelson Mandela's rise to presidency in South Africa brought a new way of thinking and restored hope among the indigenous people.

New doors opened to create lasting change in mindset and the running of community affairs in the land. It was a great honour that the LORD chose me to pray in this change alongside other intercessors in President Mandela's motherland.

Left: *Worship and prayer go hand in hand as the Holy Spirit leads.*

Left: *I travelled with Br. Joshua Okade (left, in white and black t-shirt) to Mafeking in South Africa. Pastor Thabalala's children are with us. I am 3rd right in blue.*

We used to pray with Br. Joshua in London. Today he is married with two children.

Revival broke and the church was filled to overflowing. There were lots of youth at the revival events. Among them was a former drug user from London whose life was changed forever when he met with Christ in South Africa. We were encouraged to see God move powerfully in the young man's life.

When God told me to pack my bags and go to South Africa, there was no way in the natural because my passport had been stamped '*All countries except South Africa.*'

Crying and confused, a South African pastor met me and asked what was wrong. The LORD worked through this Man of God, a stranger who invited me to his church.

Shortly after the South African embassy in Uganda cancelled the caveat and gave me a new visa that allowed me to go to South Africa. My accommodation was also sorted for the trip. A friend in London paid my ticket and took me shopping for my trip. This is how the LORD works to favour us when we obey Him!

God manifested His glory during the meeting when the pastor asked me to preach. I shared the vision God had shown me before attending the conference and the congregation were transformed from weeping to laughter. When my mission in that land was complete, the LORD asked me to return to my country and I willingly obeyed.

As God gave me instructions one by one, everything fell into place. Later when God instructed me to go to seven countries in Africa, I felt very unworthy. Why would God choose me, an unknown youth who had spent many years living in a pastor's house and serving his family?

Preaching in Gaborone, Botswana

We had a powerful revival in Botswana where I visited in 1998-99. Pastor John Morgthose hosted me. We witnessed many miracles; many people gave their lives to Christ as deliverance and spiritual healing flowed.

As anointing oil flowed from the palms of my hands; everyone who touched them was healed instantly by the power of the Holy Spirit. All glory and honour be to the LORD Most High!

Below: *I preached in Botswana while the young lady interpreted for me.*

Meanwhile, the enemy was not pleased about the breakthroughs in Botswana and sought to frustrate my onward journey.

On my way back home to Uganda after a successful mission in Botswana my suitcase was stolen. I lost all my preaching resources including videos, tapes, and other personal effects. The airline later rang me from Nigeria to inform me that they had found my suitcase. Sadly, several decades later, I have still not been reunited with my belongings.

However, such challenges have not deterred me from faithfully following the Holy Spirit's unction to serve God wherever He sends me.

Chapter Three: **God's Protection**

The Book of Ruth displays God's enduring love and commitment to honour His children who seek Him and obey Him. Ruth 4:13-17 (NIV) records how Naomi gains a son from her daughter-in-law, following the loss of her two sons.

> *So Boaz took Ruth and she became his wife. When he made love to her, the Lord enabled her to conceive, and she gave birth to a son. The women said to Naomi: "Praise be to the Lord, who this day has not left you without a guardian-redeemer. May he become famous throughout Israel! He will renew your life and sustain you in your old age. For your daughter-in-law, who loves you and who is better to you than seven sons, has given him birth." Then Naomi took the child in her arms and cared for him.* **The women living there said, "Naomi has a son!" And they named him Obed.** *He was the father of Jesse, the father of David.* (Emphasis mine)

The women rejoiced when Ruth bore a son with Boaz. They had witnessed Naomi's grief when she returned without her husband or two sons. Through her obedience and hardworking nature, Ruth had done her mother-in-law proud.

Ruth and Boaz play active roles in the marriage of Naomi's daughter-in-law. Boaz is Naomi's kinsman. After the birth of baby Obed, the women of Bethlehem say to Naomi, *"Naomi has a son"* (Ruth 4:17). New life to foster and nourish has come to her in Bethlehem.

The call to ministry involves identifying our own Bethlehem, the place where God lives. This is where He fosters and nourishes His own. Naomi travelled back to Bethlehem from Moab, expecting to find the pure Jewish life she had previously experienced when her husband and sons were alive. Her previously tranquil life was a far cry from the famine that caused her family to relocate to Moab in search of greener pastures. However, when she returned as a widow filled with deep hurt, the inhabitants of her homeland barely recognised her.

A Moabite woman is someone normally considered to be of no significance both to the public and serving in God's Kingdom. This was a key element for Naomi to bring the Moabite woman.

All this comes to fruition during harvest time. There is a harvest for every call to ministry. The favour of God fell on Ruth when she met with Boaz, as we learn in Ruth 2:8-12:

> *Then Boaz said to Ruth, "You will listen, my daughter, will you not? Do not go to glean in another field, nor go from here, but stay close by my young women. Let your eyes be on the field which they reap, and go after them. Have I not commanded the young men not to touch you?*

And when you are thirsty, go to the vessels and drink from what the young men have drawn." So she fell on her face, bowed down to the ground, and said to him, "Why have I found favor in your eyes, that you should take notice of me, since I am a foreigner?" And Boaz answered and said to her, "It has been fully reported to me, all that you have done for your mother-in-law since the death of your husband, and how you have left your father and your mother and the land of your birth, and have come to a people whom you did not know before. **The Lord repay your work, and a full reward be given you by the Lord God of Israel, under whose wings you have come for refuge.***" (Emphasis mine)*

When Boaz asked Ruth not to go away but to stay and work with his servant girls, he was protecting her. He recognised her sacrificial service to her mother-in-law Naomi since her husband's death. Boaz went further to bless Ruth who had found favour in his eyes.

What is God's call upon your life?

Every one of us is called to something special. The key is to discover the purpose of God's call upon your life.

The call of God brings favour wherever you go even if you are a foreigner. Boaz said to Ruth: *Stay with my workers until they finish harvesting all the grain.* He identified a particular gift in Ruth and sought to protect her and provide for her mother-in-law to whom she was devoted. Boaz honoured Ruth's singular devotion.

The call involves learning a new perspective like a seed plunging into the darkness of soil, for example being detained in a foreign land. Life is uncertain when one is plunged into an unknown land with different customs, a new language and way of life.

The call involves the disintegration of our initial thoughts and plans. When God steps into our life situations everything else must bow to His awesome plan, purpose and timing.

The call requires us to play our part as we allow others to play their role. It is not a simple transaction between the individual and God.

The call involves a time of waiting and worrying. Instead of worry, stay in faith, knowing that God will make good His Word in due season. He works in times and seasons.

The call brings new life and new possibilities as pure gifts. Remain in correct position in your calling and you will reap the benefits at the right time.

The call depends on a relationship with those normally considered to be unsuitable for direct involvement in making the Kingdom.

The call involves listening to the Voice of God. Naomi returned to her people as a fully loaded energetic, aggressive, combative person.

The call needs obedience which is better than sacrifice. To fulfil the call, you must listen to your senior just as Ruth listened to her mother in law Naomi. Ruth's obedience connected her to her 'kinsman redeemer' Boaz.

The call to ministry: Within our communities, we should not change to become different people in this modern world where progress is such a dominant force.

Chapter Four: Shift Your Focus

There is a human tendency to believe that the grass is always greener somewhere else. However, in the Book of Ruth, Elimelech's widow Naomi challenges us to look closer to home for clues about ministry.

When Ruth left her country to follow her mother-in-law, she had no way of knowing if the outcome would be better than what she had left in her homeland. Yet because of her loyalty to her mother-in-law, Ruth found favour even in a foreign land.

Rather than sit idly at home feeling sorry for herself and her plight, Ruth decided to act. She was loyal to her mother-in-law and sought her wise counsel.

Despite not knowing anyone in the land she had relocated to, Ruth went out and began working on Boaz's field. Soon her focus, hard work and obedience to her mother-in-law's advice landed Ruth her miracle.

Obeying the Spirit of the Lord and our leaders

Patience: God often seems to work slowly or indirectly. Although we may know the happy ending of this story, we should not forget the terrible anguish of waiting, not knowing what would happen next. As the two women waited for their breakthrough, fear replaced hope as they prayed for a breakthrough. Ruth's action was an integral part of the process of waiting in faith.

The large part of Naomi's journey to perceiving her real ministry. Oftentimes, goals dominate our thoughts as we consider ministry as baptised believers in God.

The struggle and the waiting are equally important factors.

God's timing requires our attentiveness and faith which appear too hard and bleak to comprehend. Often, things don't seem to make sense, even though we may perceive that there is more to come.

New Life and Bereavement

New life comes through loss of familiar surroundings, familiar families and familiar people. Naomi's feelings play an important part in ruth's life and story because she was able to express her bitterness and frustration. Jesus said that if we follow Him, we will carry our cross. Naomi managed to carry her own cross.

Her determination to rise from desolation brought her back to her kinsmen and women. She found solace in her homeland. Naomi's daughter-in-law gave her comfort and strength that would not have been present if Naomi had returned to Bethlehem on her own.

Interdependence: Naomi could only fulfil her individual calling by working with and giving space to others. Ministry should never isolate us, rather it should put us in deeper relationship with others. We learn this important lesson from the following passage where apostle Paul writes in 1 Corinthians 12:12-14,

12 Just as a body, though one, has many parts, but all its many parts form one body, so it is with Christ. 13 For we were all baptized by one Spirit so as to form one body—whether Jews or Gentiles, slave or free—and we were all given the one Spirit to drink. 14 Even so the body is not made up of one part but of many.

Faithfulness: we must continue to trust in God and others, however forsaken or unfulfilled we may feel. God demonstrated His amazing grace and compassion for Naomi's family by producing a son for Naomi after the death of her own sons through the Moabites.

Discernment: There is a place for being passive as well as being active, both in discernment and in the practice of ministry.

Chapter Five: Mission Calling

Sometimes God sends us to unexpected places to teach us specific life lessons. Our obedience determines the success of the mission. When we choose to listen to His Voice and act upon His instructions in a timely manner, God backs us up and provides every resource and destiny helper alongside ensuring our daily protection. Obedience is better than sacrifice (1 Samuel 15:22).

Often when we are slow to obey the Voice of the LORD, He causes situations to draw our attention to Him. This is what happened when I ended up incarcerated at Her Majesty's pleasure in England.

At the Detention Centre

On 11th January 2015 I was detained after my visa to remain in the UK which was stamped on my Ugandan Passport expired. The prison detention centre was a worrying time where my faith was tested. I learnt to wait on God for Divine intervention while in this storm.

On 2nd February 2015 at 12:30, the Holy Spirit clearly instructed me to pray for the British Prime Minister. At first, I felt uneasy. Unable to settle, I tried to sleep, sit or move around. I wanted to eat but nothing helped.

The Bible tells us to pray for our leaders, yet it is difficult to obey when one is in such a place. On the one hand you want to act on the instruction to pray for the Prime Minister when the same government is telling you to leave their country. Our God is a loving God who knows all things.

My body started behaving strangely. Unable to sleep although the room was hot with heaters on, my body felt very cold in my room in Yarlswood prison in England. My mouth was sore and I felt sick. I started praying and commanding sickness to leave my body. Feeling sicker in that I asked God why all these sicknesses had come upon me. God reminded me of His instruction to do His work in England. After I repented God miraculously healed my body.

It is always best to obey God's instruction because delaying or disobeying the Holy Spirit creates undesirable challenges.

Mission in Korea

One day the LORD impressed upon my heart to go and minister to the brethren in Korea. I was welcomed by pastor Youngi Cho and his wife at the Soul Yoido Full Gospel Church in South Korea.

Above: *With Pastor Youngi Cho's wife at their church foyer.*

The people of South Korea are very warm and kind. The country is very beautiful with striking buildings. Below, I am standing on the steps of the capital city of Yoido.

 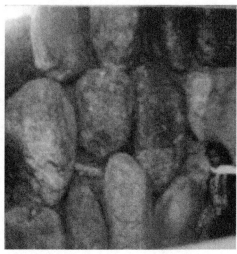

Above Left: *At Yoido Full Gospel Church, South Korea.*
Above Right: *On the Prayer Mountain next to the Church.*

The interior of the church is very spacious. Indeed, when the praises go up, the LORD manifests His glory upon the worshippers.

I was taken to South Korea by faith. My ticket cost $2,500. This was a big deal because I had never touched such a huge amount of money in my life. We went to pray at the South Korea Prayer Mountain with my kind and welcoming hosts.

The climb up to the mountain was steep; my heart filled with gratitude once we arrived safely at the top. I believe God heard my earnest prayers of intercession and thanksgiving on that day.

My experience in South Korea taught me to trust God fully because He is dependable. When we pray to Him, God promises to supply all our needs according to His glorious riches in Christ Jesus.

Ministry in the Democratic Republic of Congo

I visited the Democratic Republic of Congo at a time when the country was experiencing civil war. We travelled in pickups which were detailed to carry food. We passed through dangerous forests; along the way we encountered numerous roadblocks manned by the militia. One needed to have $10 ready to hand over to the officials before being allowed to proceed on the journey.

Revival came to the land shortly after we prayed for Congo where we also witnessed visible changes and manifestations. The leader who had declared himself life president passed away within two weeks. It was amazing to be relieved from the dreaded roadblocks on our return journey to Uganda. I was grateful for the unexpected favour of being transported back to the Congo/Uganda border of Kasese in an armoured army van. God surely protects and honours His own when we diligently seek Him and heed His Word and impeccable timing!

Chapter Six: **Call to Ministry Biblical Examples**

Let us examine some unique examples of men and women who heeded Go's call to showcase God's glory around the world. First, Mary the mother of our LORD Jesus Christ who was a teenager when her destiny was revealed in a most unusual way.

Mary's Prophetic Call and Obedience

It was not easy for Mary who was to become the mother of our LORD Jesus to accept God's call upon her life (read Luke chapter 1). She was planning to get married to a certain carpenter named Joseph after which they would get on with the business of living within a normal family structure. Little did she know that history was about to be transformed by the power of the Holy Spirit?

Imagine an angel suddenly appearing before you with an out-of-this-world greeting followed by a transformational declaration concerning your life's mission.

How would you react? Would you laugh like Abraham's wife Sarah, or doubt like Zechariah did when the angel appeared to tell him that he would father a son (John the Baptist) who would turn the hearts of the fathers to their sons? This prophecy would require a miracle and deep faith since both Zechariah and Elizabeth were past child-bearing age. Yet God never makes mistakes. His Word is *Yes* and *Amen* in Christ.

Suddenly an angel appeared to Mary, interrupting her thoughts with a most unusual greeting: *"**Rejoice, highly favored one, the Lord is with you; blessed are you among women!**"* (Luke 1:28). The angel dispelled Mary's fears, after which he continued,

> *"**Do not be afraid, Mary, for you have found favor with God. And behold, you will conceive in your womb and bring forth a Son, and shall call His name Jesus. He will be great, and will be called the Son of the Highest;** and the Lord God will give Him the throne of His father David. ... **and of His kingdom there will be no end.**"* (v30-33)

Mary answered, *"**How will that be, since I do not know a man?**"* (Luke 1:34) The angel continued (v35-37):

> ...*"**The Holy Spirit will come upon you, and the power of the Highest will overshadow you; therefore, also, that Holy One who is to be born will be called the Son of God.** Now indeed, Elizabeth your relative has also conceived a son in her old age; and this is now the sixth month for her who was called barren. **For with God nothing will be impossible.**"*

By revealing that Elizabeth was also with child, the angel affirmed that God could do what was considered impossible from a human perspective.

Mary believed and said, *"**Behold the maidservant of the Lord! Let it be to me according to your word.**"*

As Mary pondered these secrets in her heart, her divine purpose and destiny on earth was confirmed through her miraculous pregnancy.

When a woman is pregnant the symptoms of a child are revealed in the stomach. As soon as Elizabeth greeted Mary the mother of Jesus, the baby in Mary's womb leapt for joy. After observing Mary's quiet faith, Elizabeth declared (v45), *"Blessed is she who believed, for there will be a fulfillment of those things which were told her from the Lord."*

We are blessed when we take God at His Word and trust that He will accomplish what He says concerning us along our earthly mission. After believing God, Mary started praising Him.

Mary's song of praise acknowledges her gratitude and wonder at being chosen to bring forth the holy Child. *My soul rejoices in the Lord my savour, the Lord and my Spirit rejoices in God my salvation...* (see v46-55). Surely the Mighty One has done great things. Let us emulate Mary who humbly and uncomplainingly accepted God's call upon her life, and faithfully moved forward with it.

Mary demonstrated her great faith in God at a young innocent age. Despite not knowing all the ins and outs of how the angel's declaration would unfold in her life, or how the trajectory of her life would dramatically change, she chose to obey God, pray and praise Him for His amazing promise. Mary had no idea how those in her community and family would perceive her. Regardless, she patiently pondered the promise in her heart.

The Word of God is speaking to you as you read this book. God is reminding you that before you were born, He knew you and called you a prophet to the nations.

Jeremiah's Calling

The Lord God has put the His Word on your lips; He has also put you in charge over kingdoms and nations. God has given you the power to uproot, to pulldown, to destroy and to tear down in pieces, to build and to plant. There is a profound revelation recorded in Jeremiah 1:5-12 below. Consider Jeremiah's response when God called him to the nations.

> *"**Before I formed you in the womb I knew you; before you were born I sanctified you; I ordained you a prophet to the nations.**" Then said I: "Ah, Lord God! Behold, I cannot speak, for I am a youth." But the Lord said to me: "Do not say, 'I am a youth,' For you shall go to all to whom I send you, and whatever I command you, you shall speak. **Do not be afraid of their faces, for I am with you to deliver you,**" says the Lord. Then the Lord put forth His hand and touched my mouth, and the Lord said to me: "**Behold, I have put My words in your mouth. See, I have this day set you over the nations and over the kingdoms, to root out and to pull down, to destroy and to throw down, to build and to plant.**"*

*Moreover the word of the Lord came to me, saying, "Jeremiah, what do you see?" And I said, "I see a branch of an almond tree." Then the Lord said to me, **"You have seen well, for I am ready to perform My word.**" (Emphasis mine)*

God's Word is unwaveringly true, timely and consistent. Everything He says concerning your life is linked to His predestined promise for you. Commit to taking His Word seriously and following through on what He instructs you to do; the benefits are well worth it.

Time to reflect:

God's Word is His will for your life. Will you choose today to fully obey His Word and trust His heart concerning what He has called you to?

Chapter Seven: **God's Prophetic Call**

Let us now consider: Who is a prophet and what does a prophet do?

Since the office of a prophet is very significant in life and ministry, prophetic gifts must be encouraged to grow and flourish within the body of Christ.

Who is a prophet?

He or she is an encourager who exhorts and strengthens the church.

He is also a builder who nourishes disciples' lives. A prophet never tears down. If you are a disciple of Jesus Christ, you must be willing to grow and mature in Him.

A prophet's message may sound harsh and touch raw nerves that may affect both mature and immature Christians. Believers need to be willing to grow and be nurtured into spiritual maturity as children of God. Prophets of God are also priests who portray Christ's character.

God often called on prophets to lay hands on kings or priests, singling them out for leadership and authority in their kingly or priestly office. Examples include Samuel anointing David when he was tending sheep in his father's farm (1 Samuel 16:1-13). Prophets were essential for restoring the keys of power in the Old Testament.

The prophetic office may come across as being critical. Although it may cause friction, it is designed to set a high standard for all believers. In Bible times prophets were held in high regard and were required to uphold high moral standards. Examples include Samuel, Moses and Elijah.

Moses parted the Red Sea, creating room for the children of Israel to cross safely to enter the wilderness as they made their way to the Promised Land (Ex.14:13-23).

Prophet Elijah walked closely with God and heard God audibly call him to service. He heard the sound of rain before it became visible (1 Kings 18:44). Elijah also saw a cloud before anyone else saw it. On one occasion Elijah called for fire from heaven to consume wickedness on earth (1 Kings 18:21).

One day God told Elijah to hide from an enemy (1 Kings 17:2-3). Elijah's body was also transformed ensuring that he was not subject to sickness, death or physical pain (2 Kings 2:11).

Pray the following verses and ask God to hide you in the shelter of His wings. (Ps.17:8; Ps. 31:20; Ps.32:7). Today God is calling His prophets to hide under the shadow of His wings so that we can receive individual attention and instruction from the LORD.

Prayer is the believer's weapon of faith which yields results. Elijah depended wholly on God alone.

In 1 Kings 17 Elijah decreed drought in the Name of the Living God. The God of Israel whom we serve keeps His Covenant (see also Isaiah 28:31; 2 Timothy 4:7; Daniel 11:32).

God's mighty acts are revealed through prophets of faith. For example, Elijah dried the waters of the Jordan (1 Kings 17:1-2), then hid by the Brook Cherith and was fed by ravens (17:3-7). The widow who was getting ready to prepare her final meal for her son received God's mercy and long life was extended to them because of her obedience. Instead of complaining when Elijah asked her to prepare him some bread with the remaining flour and oil the widow served Elijah. As a result of her selfless action, her bottles of oil never ran dry. She was then able to sell most of the oil and get enough money to sustain her family (1 Kings 17:8-16).

Elijah raised the widow's son (v17-24); he later called down fire from heaven to consume the sacrifice in the presence of the false prophets of Baal (1 Kings 18:36-39). At the end of his ministry Elijah was raptured into the whirlwind by a chariot of fire into the presence of God (2 Kings 2:11).

In 2 Kings 19:12 prophet Isaiah interceded for king Hezekiah and delivered a word of victory through the king's messengers. Never give up. God is ready to work with you. When He calls you be sure to answer: *Here I am, LORD, send me* as in the following examples.

Consider prophet Moses's lifestyle and calling. Moses was born and abandoned into the river to save his life from certain death after the wicked ruler passed a decree to find and murder all male babies under the age of two.

Moses was born with a mark of protection (Ex. 2:3); he floated in a basket and did not drown. The name 'Moses' means 'deliverer' or 'saviour'.

Let us examine Moses' credentials. After running away from a sheltered and favoured life as a prince of Egypt, Moses worked as a shepherd in his father-in-law's farm. Moses probably stuttered (Ex. 4:10, 3:4), yet God had called him to demonstrate His Power. He heard God's call through the burning bush, and responded, *Here I am LORD, send me.* When Moses suffered the dreaded leprosy disease (Ex.4:6-8) God demonstrated His Power and healed him instantly.

God wrote the Ten Commandments on clay tablets and gave them to Moses to deliver to the people (Ex. 24:4, 9-11); this was a great privilege; God also spoke to Moses face to face.

Moses was the humblest man on the face of the earth (Num.12:3). He died at the age of 120 years, full of strength with clear sight (Deut. 34:7). Moses was buried on the mountain and his grave was never found.

Samuel became a great prophet who foretold many truths on what the LORD was about to do. When he heard God's Voice asking, *Whom shall I send, and who will go for Us?* Isaiah replied: *Here am I! Send me.* (Is. 6:8)

When the angel of God called Jacob in a dream, he responded, *Here I am.* (Gen. 31:11) God saved the nation through Joseph when he moved his entire family to Egypt, to escape the famine.

Hebrews 13:8 declares that *Jesus Christ is the same yesterday, today and forever.* Let us therefore offer through Jesus a continual sacrifice of praise to God, proclaiming our allegiance to His Name.

Chapter Eight: Rising Above Spiritual Adversity

The enemy does not like it when God singles you out for His glory. Expect spiritual attacks aimed at causing delay or derailment of your Divine purpose. This is why we must be alert and wise to the enemy's ploys and hidden agendas. He is called the deceiver and will do anything possible to try and remove God's chosen eons from fulling destiny. Do not let that happen to you my beloved in the Lord.

"What can we do when we face spiritual attack?"

The first thing to do when we believe we may be under a spiritual attack is to determine, as far as possible, whether what we are experiencing is truly a spiritual attack from demonic forces or simply the effects of living in a sin-cursed world. Some people blame every sin, every conflict, and every problem on demons they believe need to be cast out.

Apostle Paul instructs Christians to wage war against the sin in themselves (Romans 6) and to wage war against the evil one (Ephesians 6:10-18). The battle plan is the same whether we are experiencing spiritual attack from demonic forces or just battling the evil within ourselves and that which inhabits the world.

The key to the battle plan is found in Ephesians 6:10-18. Paul begins by saying that we must *be strong in the Lord and in His power*, not in our own power which is no match for the devil and his forces. Paul then exhorts us to *put on the armour of God*, which is the only way to take a stand against spiritual attacks. In our own strength and power, we have no chance of defeating the *"spiritual forces of evil in the heavenly realms"* (v12). Only the *"full armour of God"* will equip us to withstand spiritual attack. We can only be strong in the Lord's power because only God's armour protects us, and our battle is against spiritual forces of evil in the world.

With the description of the spiritual armour God gives us, the good news is that these things are readily available to all who belong to Christ. We are to *stand firm with the belt of truth*, buckle *on the breastplate of righteousness*, wear on our feet *the gospel of peace*, hold up *the shield of faith*, wear *the helmet of salvation*, and wield *the sword of the Spirit*, which is **the Word of God**—the only offensive weapon in the whole armoury. The rest are defensive.

Reflect on what each of these pieces of spiritual armour represent and how you can apply them in spiritual warfare.

We are to speak the truth against Satan's lies. We are to rest in the fact that we are declared righteous because of Christ's sacrifice for us. We are to proclaim the gospel no matter how much resistance we receive. We are not to waver in our faith, no matter how fiercely we are attacked.

Our ultimate defence is the assurance we have of our salvation, an assurance that no spiritual force can take away. Our offensive weapon is the Word of God, not our own opinions and feelings. Finally, we are to follow Jesus' example in recognizing that some spiritual victories are only possible through prayer.

Jesus is our ultimate example when it comes to warding off spiritual attacks. Observe how Jesus handled direct attacks from Satan when He was tempted by him in the wilderness.

Matthew 4:1-11 demonstrates how Jesus answered every temptation in the same way—with the words "*It is written*" and a quote from the Scriptures. Jesus knew the Word of the living God is the most powerful weapon against the temptations of the devil. If Jesus Himself used the Word to counter the devil, do we dare to use anything less?

The ultimate example of how *not* to engage in spiritual warfare is seen in the experience of the seven sons of Sceva, a Jewish priest. The sons went around driving out evil spirits by trying to invoke the name of the Lord Jesus over those who were demon-possessed.

> *Then some of the itinerant Jewish exorcists took it upon themselves to call the name of the Lord Jesus over those who had evil spirits, saying, "We exorcise you by the Jesus whom Paul preaches." Also there were seven sons of Sceva, a Jewish chief priest, who did so. And the evil spirit answered and said, "**Jesus I know, and Paul I know; but who are you?**"*

Then the man in whom the evil spirit was leaped on them, overpowered them, and prevailed against them, so that they fled out of that house naked and wounded. ***This became known both to all Jews and Greeks dwelling in Ephesus; and fear fell on them all, and the name of the Lord Jesus was magnified.*** (Emphasis mine)

The seven sons of Scarva were using Jesus' Name, but because they did not have a relationship with Jesus, their words were void of any power or authority. They were not relying on Jesus as their Lord and Saviour, neither did they apply the Word of God in their spiritual warfare. As a result, they received a humiliating beating. May we learn from their bad example and conduct spiritual warfare as the Bible instructs. Deuteronomy 1:8 reveals,

See, I have set the land before you; go in and possess the land which the Lord swore to your fathers—to Abraham, Isaac, and Jacob—to give to them and their descendants after them.'

Fellowship within the church community is vital to enhancing spiritual growth and support. Consider who you call for spiritual backup when you need someone to stand in the gap and agree with you in prayer. If you are not connected with a spirit-filled body of Christ, you may get overwhelmed when the battle gets fierce.

I thank God for my church family; together we nourish and intercede for one another, maintaining the powerful bond of Christian love, unity and fellowship.

Above: *My husband Pastor Simon Anderson (left, standing) with Reverend Terence Brimson (seated, holding my hand), Reverend John Hodgetts and me (right, standing) with other church members at the Great Awakening in 2015.*

These are some of God's Generals who have fought in the spiritual and physical arenas. We often fellowship with partner ministries in various physical locations where iron sharpens iron. This is in addition to our online fellowship which joins people from all walks of life and is accessible globally.

Christ called us to preach the gospel to every nation and all people; We are grateful for the technology He has provided to make this possible when we are not travelling across the globe.

Above: *After service with some members of Power of The Word Ministries led by Pastor Osborn (centre) and family.*

A perfect example of how the Church should walk in love. John 15:3-17 teaches us how to love one another by following Christ's perfect example.

> *You are already clean because of the word which I have spoken to you. Abide in Me, and I in you. As the branch cannot bear fruit of itself, unless it abides in the vine, neither can you, unless you abide in Me. "I am the vine, you are the branches. He who abides in Me, and I in him, bears much fruit; for without Me you can do nothing.*

If anyone does not abide in Me, he is cast out as a branch and is withered; and they gather them and throw them into the fire, and they are burned. If you abide in Me, and My words abide in you, you will ask what you desire, and it shall be done for you. By this My Father is glorified, that you bear much fruit; so you will be My disciples. "As the Father loved Me, I also have loved you; abide in My love. If you keep My commandments, you will abide in My love, just as I have kept My Father's commandments and abide in His love.

Following Jesus Christ's blueprint of love in our daily Christian walk will create more joy, peace and harmony in our lives, our homes, our ministries and communities. The consequence of disobedience is removal from the Vine (v7). However, Jesus promises to grant our requests as we remain in relationship with Him. Hearing and heeding His Word will protect us from falling, and our branches will not be disconnected from the Vine.

"These things I have spoken to you, that My joy may remain in you, and that your joy may be full. This is My commandment, that you love one another as I have loved you. Greater love has no one than this, than to lay down one's life for his friends. You are My friends if you do whatever I command you. No longer do I call you servants, for a servant does not know what his master is doing; but I have called you friends, for all things that I heard from My Father I have made known to you.

You did not choose Me, but I chose you and appointed you that you should go and bear fruit, and that your fruit should remain, that whatever you ask the Father in My name He may give you. These things I command you, that you love one another.

Verses 11-17 solidify Christ's great love and commitment to protect His friends who abide in Him. What a blessing to be called *friends* by the One whose nature is LOVE!

John 15:18-25 describes the world's hatred of followers of Christ.

If you were of the world, the world would love its own. Yet because you are not of the world, but I chose you out of the world, therefore the world hates you. Remember the word that I said to you, 'A servant is not greater than his master.' If they persecuted Me, they will also persecute you. If they kept My word, they will keep yours also. But all these things they will do to you for My name's sake, because they do not know Him who sent Me. If I had not come and spoken to them, they would have no sin, but now they have no excuse for their sin. He who hates Me hates My Father also. If I had not done among them the works which no one else did, they would have no sin; but now they have seen and also hated both Me and My Father. But this happened that the word might be fulfilled which is written in their law, 'They hated Me without a cause.'

Finally, in verses 26-27 Jesus also foretold the rejection that would face believers in days to come.

> *"But when the Helper comes, whom I shall send to you from the Father, the Spirit of truth who proceeds from the Father, He will testify of Me. And you also will bear witness, because you have been with Me from the beginning.*

Let us rejoice and thank God for sending us the Holy Spirit who helps and strengthens us in weakness and guides us in all Truth.

Isaiah 49:1-13 and 15-23 describe the role of the servant who is the light to the gentiles.

> *"Listen, O coastlands, to Me, and take heed, you peoples from afar! The Lord has called Me from the womb; from the matrix of My mother He has made mention of My name. And He has made My mouth like a sharp sword; in the shadow of His hand He has hidden Me, and made Me a polished shaft; in His quiver He has hidden Me." "And He said to me, 'You are My servant, O Israel, in whom I will be glorified.' Then I said, 'I have labored in vain, I have spent my strength for nothing and in vain; yet surely my just reward is with the Lord, and my work with my God.' " "And now the Lord says, Who formed Me from the womb to be His Servant, to bring Jacob back to Him, so that Israel is gathered to Him (For I shall be*

glorious in the eyes of the Lord, and My God shall be My strength), Indeed He says, 'It is too small a thing that You should be My Servant to raise up the tribes of Jacob, and to restore the preserved ones of Israel; I will also give You as a light to the Gentiles, that You should be My salvation to the ends of the earth.' "

Thus says the Lord, the Redeemer of Israel, their Holy One, to Him whom man despises, To Him whom the nation abhors, to the Servant of rulers: "Kings shall see and arise, Princes also shall worship, because of the Lord who is faithful, the Holy One of Israel; and He has chosen You." Thus says the Lord: "In an acceptable time I have heard You, and in the day of salvation I have helped You; I will preserve You and give You as a covenant to the people, to restore the earth, to cause them to inherit the desolate heritages. That You may say to the prisoners, 'Go forth,' to those who are in darkness, 'Show yourselves.' "They shall feed along the roads, and their pastures shall be on all desolate heights. They shall neither hunger nor thirst, neither heat nor sun shall strike them; for He who has mercy on them will lead them, even by the springs of water He will guide them.

I will make each of My mountains a road, and My highways shall be elevated. Surely these shall come from afar; Look! Those from the north and the west, and these from the land of Sinim." Sing, O heavens! Be joyful, O earth! And break out in singing, O mountains! For the Lord has comforted His people, and will have mercy on His afflicted.

When God calls us into service in His Vineyard, He provides the resources and opportunities to minister to His flock. He is committed to remember Zion (v15-16, 25-26).

"Can a woman forget her nursing child, and not have compassion on the son of her womb? Surely they may forget, yet I will not forget you. 16 See, I have inscribed you on the palms of My hands; your walls are continually before Me. *...But thus says the Lord: ...* **for I will contend with him who contends with you, and I will save your children.** *...All flesh shall know that I, the Lord, am your Savior, and your Redeemer, the Mighty One of Jacob."* (Emphasis mine)

Declaration:

Behold, what manner of love the Father has bestowed upon His beloved children! Continuous divine protection is our portion in Christ Jesus our Lord and Redeemer.

Chapter Nine: **Standing in the Gap: Biblical Examples**

The following stories will encourage you that God can use anyone to fulfil His express purpose. This may involve repositioning someone in a different land, changing jobs or identity, uplifting to high office or any other redefining as needed. The only requirements are: the individual's willingness, focus and commitment to obey the Voice of God.

Nehemiah's Calling

In Nehemiah 1:4 we read how the prophet was deeply burdened for his people and for God's work in Judah. For four months Nehemiah tearfully poured out his heart to God in fasting and prayer because of the trouble afflicting God's people. He confessed the sins of his people, reminding God of His Word. When Sanballat and Tobias taunted God (Nehemiah chapter 4), the Almighty stepped in and defended His honour, saving His people from shame and ruin. In Nehemiah 4:!4, Nehemiah instructed his people:

> *And I looked, and arose and said to the nobles, to the leaders, and to the rest of the people, "Do not be afraid of them. Remember the Lord, great and awesome, and fight for your brethren, your sons, your daughters, your wives, and your houses."*

God heard His children's petition and gave Nehemiah wisdom on how to defend their city and complete their mission of rebuilding the wall.

Nehemiah 13 records how revival broke through. The principle of separation from ungodly practices and followers is revealed in this passage.

Food is very important (v2). Instead of meeting the Israelites with food, they called Balaam to curse them. However, in His mercy God turned the curse into a blessing.

Prayer:

May the Lord our God turn every curse into a blessing, in our income, our families our jobs, and in our lives.

We decree that every curse is broken from our lives, our children, our neighbourhood and our nation in Jesus' mighty Name.

We break every curse that has been pronounced over us in the Mighty Name of Jesus.

Nehemiah was a builder Let us build together instead of breaking what is being built. We often judge what we see we our brothers and sisters doing. Focus on building a team not a one-man show.

Nehemiah was a man of conviction (v9). He gave orders to purify the rooms and then return the equipment of the house of God along with grain offerings and incense. Meanwhile, all the Levites and singers had gone back to their own fields.

Why is the house of God neglected? (Neh.13:11) *"Then I called the leaders to gather and stationed them at their posts."* When the house of God is not in order people bring sparingly. (v12) *All Judah brought the tithe and offerings of grain, new wine into the storerooms.* Nehemiah further appointed five faithful treasurers to watch over the storehouse and distribute supplies to their brethren.

Nehemiah restored full worship in the temple along with the Levite ministers and singers. As a result, the people were able to bring their tithes and offerings and people were more able to tithe when they worshipped God which in turn brought blessings. That was when God raised Malachi. Tithing is a blessing for those who are faithful to serving God. It is not based on law.

Let us ask God to remember our service, like Nehemiah did in chapter 13:14:

Prayer:

LORD God, remember me and show me Your mercy according to Your great love. Remember me with favour, oh my God.

Remember me, O my God, concerning this, and do not wipe out my good deeds that I have done for the house of my God, and for its services! (v14)

Father God, remember me in whatever I have ever done for You.

May. God reward you and use you for His glory.

Queen Esther's Calling

Do you know God's mission for your life? Esther was commissioned to save the Jewish people from evil decrees. She was favoured and chosen as queen to succeed Vashti who had fallen out of the king's favour after disobeying him (read Esther chapters 1 and 2).

A time of favour is not your time to rejoice and make merry. It is a time to standing in the gap and intercede on behalf of those who are less able.

Read the following account of Queen Esther and Mordecai. An enemy of the Jews named Haman had built gallows and deceived the king to sign a decree that would have all the Jews who did not obey the contents of the edict to be put to death. Unknown to King Xerxes, his queen Esther was a Jew. This meant that she would also suffer the same fate as her fellow kinsmen unless she risked her life to appear before the king without being summoned.

Esther 4:5-17 details how Esther agreed to help the Jews.

So Esther's maids and eunuchs came and told her, and the queen was deeply distressed. Then she sent garments to clothe Mordecai and take his sackcloth away from him, but he would not accept them.

Then Esther called Hathach, one of the king's eunuchs whom he had appointed to attend her, and she gave him a command concerning Mordecai, to learn what and why this was. So Hathach went out to Mordecai in the city square that was in front of the king's gate.

And Mordecai told him all that had happened to him, and the sum of money that Haman had promised to pay into the king's treasuries to destroy the Jews. He also gave him a copy of the written decree for their destruction, which was given at Shushan, that he might show it to Esther and explain it to her, and that he might command her to go in to the king to make supplication to him and plead before him for her people. So Hathach returned and told Esther the words of Mordecai.

Then Esther spoke to Hathach, and gave him a command for Mordecai: "All the king's servants and the people of the king's provinces know that any man or woman who goes into the inner court to the king, who has not been called, he has but one law: put all to death, except the one to whom the king holds out the golden scepter, that he may live. Yet I myself have not been called to go in to the king these thirty days." So they told Mordecai Esther's words.

And Mordecai told them to answer Esther: "Do not think in your heart that you will escape in the king's palace any more than all the other Jews. For if you remain completely silent at this time, relief and deliverance will arise for the Jews from another place, but you and your father's house will perish. Yet who knows whether you have come to the kingdom for such a time as this?" Then Esther told them to reply to Mordecai: "Go, gather all the Jews who are present in Shushan, and fast for me; neither eat nor drink for three days, night or day. My maids and I will fast likewise. And so I will go to the king, which is against the law; and if I perish, I perish!" So Mordecai went his way and did according to all that Esther commanded him.

Ponder Esther's and Mordecai's actions as you complete the following reflection from this chapter.

Reflect:

Recall a time when you were asked to do something that caused you to cry out to God for mercy on behalf of a community, family member, work colleague or friend.

1. How did your faith grow because of the answered prayer?

2. What did you discover about the fruit of your obedience and selfless sacrifice?

What advice can you give to encourage a new believer who is trying to do the right thing in a hostile environment?

Chapter Ten: Hearing God: Dreams & Visions

15 After these things the word of the Lord came to Abram in a vision, saying, "Do not be afraid, Abram. I am your shield, your exceedingly great reward." (Genesis 15:1)

In this chapter we will examine Scriptural evidence from the Old and New Testaments where God communicates His heart to us through dreams and visions.

Genesis 46:2-4 - Jacob's Journey to Egypt to be reunited with his long-lost son after learning Joseph was still alive. This came when Canaan was going through a severe famine.

Then God spoke to Israel in the visions of the night, and said, "Jacob, Jacob!" And he said, "Here I am." So He said, "I am God, the God of your father; do not fear to go down to Egypt, for I will make of you a great nation there. I will go down with you to Egypt…

Whenever God gives us prophetic dreams, He follows them up with an interpretation. For example, after Pharaoh's two dreams which his magicians could not interpret, he called for Joseph to be brought up from the dingy prison and interpret them (read Genesis 41).

Genesis 41:1-7, 14-17, 25.

"Now a word was secretly brought to me, and my ear received a whisper of it. In disquieting thoughts from the visions of the night, when deep sleep falls on men, fear came upon me, and trembling, which made all my bones shake. Then a spirit passed before my face; the hair on my body stood up.

Now it happened at the end of two full years that Pharaoh had a dream, and behold, he was standing by the Nile. And lo, from the Nile there came up seven cows, sleek and fat; and they grazed in the marsh grass. Then behold, seven other cows came up after them from the Nile, ugly and gaunt, and they stood by the other cows on the bank of the Nile.

Then Pharaoh sent and called Joseph, and they brought him quickly out of the dungeon; and he shaved, changed his clothing, and came to Pharaoh. And Pharaoh said to Joseph, "I have had a dream, and there is no one who can interpret it. But I have heard it said of you that you can understand a dream, to interpret it." **So Joseph answered Pharaoh, saying, "It is not in me; God will give Pharaoh an answer of peace."** *Then Pharaoh said to Joseph: "Behold, in my dream I stood on the bank of the river. ... Then Joseph said to Pharaoh, "The dreams of Pharaoh are one;* **God has shown Pharaoh what He is about to do***: (emphasis mine).

By the time Joseph came out of prison he had learned to walk in humility before God, recognising that his gift of interpreting dreams came from God. We do well to acknowledge the gifts God gives us to empower the body of Christ.

Exodus 3:2-3. The angel of God appeared to Moses.

And the Angel of the Lord appeared to him in a flame of fire from the midst of a bush. So he looked, and behold, the bush was burning with fire, but the bush was not consumed. Then Moses said, "I will now turn aside and see this great sight, why the bush does not burn."

Judges 7:13-15. Gideon's answer comes through a man interpreting a dream.

And when Gideon had come, there was a man telling a dream to his companion. He said, "I have had a dream: To my surprise, a loaf of barley bread tumbled into the camp of Midian; it came to a tent and struck it so that it fell and overturned, and the tent collapsed." Then his companion answered and said, "This is nothing else but the sword of Gideon the son of Joash, a man of Israel! Into his hand God has delivered Midian and the whole camp." And so it was, when Gideon heard the telling of the dream and its interpretation, that he worshiped. He returned to the camp of Israel, and said, "Arise, for the Lord has delivered the camp of Midian into your hand."

Consider:

How does God speak to you? Do you know His Voice?

1 Samuel 3:2-15. Samuel learns to hear God's Voice.

It happened at that time as Eli was lying down in his place (now his eyesight had begun to grow dim and he could not see well), and the lamp of God had not yet gone out, and Samuel was lying down in the temple of the Lord where the ark of God was, that the Lord called Samuel; and he said, "Here I am."

The following passage demonstrates the importance of seeking the LORD's face about His plan. Be attentive because sometimes He will send a prophet to deliver your answer.

2 Samuel 7:4-5a, 17. God reveals His plans to David through prophet Nathan.

But it happened that night that the word of the Lord came to Nathan, saying, "Go and tell My servant David, 'Thus says the Lord:... According to all these words and according to all this vision, so Nathan spoke to David.

Read 1 Kings 3 where Solomon asks for Wisdom

When we seek the LORD in prayer and intercession, He answers us and surprises us with more than we ask for. This was King Solomon's special gift when he humbled himself before God and offered sacrifices at Gibeon.

1 Kings 3:4-6, 15.

Now the king went to Gibeon to sacrifice there, for that was the great high place: Solomon offered a thousand burnt offerings on that altar. At Gibeon the Lord appeared to Solomon in a dream by night; and God said, "Ask! What shall I give you?"

And Solomon said: "You have shown great mercy to Your servant David my father, because he walked before You in truth, in righteousness, and in uprightness of heart with You; You have continued this great kindness for him, and You have given him a son to sit on his throne, as it is this day. ... Then Solomon awoke; and indeed it had been a dream. And he came to Jerusalem and stood before the ark of the covenant of the Lord, offered up burnt offerings, offered peace offerings, and made a feast for all his servants.

Isaiah 6:1-8.

In the year of King Uzziah's death I saw the Lord sitting on a throne, lofty and exalted, with the train of His robe filling the temple. Seraphim stood above Him, each having six wings: with two he covered his face, and with two he covered his feet, and with two he flew. And one called out to another and said, "Holy, Holy, Holy, is the Lord of hosts, the whole earth is full of His glory."

Ezekiel 1:4-14.

As I looked, behold, a storm wind was coming from the north, a great cloud with fire flashing forth continually and a bright light around it, and in its midst something like glowing metal in the midst of the fire. Within it there were figures resembling four living beings. And this was their appearance: they had human form. Each of them had four faces and four wings.

God may also choose to transport one from the earthly realm into the spiritual in a vision as in the following examples.

Ezekiel 8:1-4. Ezekiel sees a vision of the abominations in the Temple.

*And it came to pass in the sixth year, in the sixth month, on the fifth day of the month, as I sat in my house with the elders of Judah sitting before me, **that the hand of the Lord God fell upon me there**. Then I looked, and there was a likeness, like the appearance of fire—from the appearance of His waist and downward, fire; and from His waist and upward, like the appearance of brightness, like the color of amber. He stretched out the form of a hand, and took me by a lock of my hair; **and the Spirit lifted me up between earth and heaven, and brought me in visions of God to Jerusalem**, to the door of the north gate of the inner court, where the seat of the image of jealousy was, which provokes to jealousy. **And behold, the glory of the God of Israel was there, like the vision that I saw in the plain**.* (Emphasis mine)

Ezekiel 11:24-25.

Then the Spirit took me up and brought me in a vision by the Spirit of God into Chaldea, to those in captivity. And the vision that I had seen went up from me. So I spoke to those in captivity of all the things the Lord had shown me.

Ezekiel 37:1-3, 9-10. Ezekiel in the Valley of Dry Bones.

The hand of the Lord was upon me, and He brought me out by the Spirit of the Lord and set me down in the middle of the valley; and it was full of bones.

He caused me to pass among them round about, and behold, there were very many on the surface of the valley; and lo, they were very dry. He said to me, "Son of man, can these bones live?" And I answered, "O Lord God, You know."... Also He said to me, "Prophesy to the breath, prophesy, son of man, and say to the [a]breath, 'Thus says the Lord God: "Come from the four winds, O breath, and breathe on these slain, that they may live." ' " So I prophesied as He commanded me, and [b]breath came into them, and they lived, and stood upon their feet, an exceedingly great army.

Daniel 2:28 – God often reveals His mysteries to His loved ones through dreams.

However, there is a God in heaven who reveals mysteries, and He has made known to King Nebuchadnezzar what will take place in the latter days. This was your dream and the visions in your mind while on your bed.

Daniel 4:5.

I saw a dream and it made me fearful; and these fantasies as I lay on my bed and the visions in my mind kept alarming me.

Daniel 2:19 - God speaks in visions.

Then the mystery was revealed to Daniel in a night vision. Then Daniel blessed the God of heaven…

Amos 7:1-9. Amos sees a series of visions.

First, the vision of the Locusts (v1-3)

Thus the Lord God showed me: Behold, He formed locust swarms at the beginning of the late crop; indeed it was the late crop after the king's mowings. And so it was, when they had finished eating the grass of the land, that I said: "O Lord God, forgive, I pray! Oh, that Jacob may stand, for he is small!" So the Lord relented concerning this. "It shall not be," said the Lord.

Next, the vision of the Fire (v4-6)

Thus the Lord God showed me: Behold, the Lord God called for conflict by fire, and it consumed the great deep and devoured the territory. Then I said: "O Lord God, cease, I pray! Oh, that Jacob may stand, for he is small!"

So the Lord relented concerning this. "This also shall not be," said the Lord God.

Finally, the vision of the Plumb Line (v7-9)

Thus He showed me: Behold, the Lord stood on a wall made with a plumb line, with a plumb line in His hand. And the Lord said to me, "Amos, what do you see?" And I said, "A plumb line." Then the Lord said: "Behold, I am setting a plumb line in the midst of My people Israel; I will not pass by them anymore. The high places of Isaac shall be desolate, and the sanctuaries of Israel shall be laid waste. I will rise with the sword against the house of Jeroboam."

Amos 8:1-6.

Thus the Lord God showed me, and behold, there was a basket of summer fruit. He said, "What do you see, Amos?" And I said, "A basket of summer fruit." Then the Lord said to me, "The end has come for My people Israel. I will spare them no longer. The songs of the palace will turn to wailing in that day," declares the Lord God. "Many will be the corpses; in every place they will cast them forth in silence."

Amos 9:1.

I saw the Lord standing by the altar, and He said: "Strike the doorposts, that the thresholds may shake, and break them on the heads of them all. I will slay the last of them with the sword. He who flees from them shall not get away, and he who escapes from them shall not be delivered.

Zechariah 1:8. Can you see the mysteries of the kingdom of God?

I saw at night, and behold, a man was riding on a red horse, and he was standing among the myrtle trees which were in the ravine, with red, sorrel and white horses behind him.

Zechariah 3:1. The devil is the accuser of the brethren. Thank God for sending Jesus to die on the Cross. When He resurrected He overcame the devil by the Blood of the Lamb.

Then he showed me Joshua the high priest standing before the angel of the Lord, and Satan standing at his right hand to accuse him.

There is a close connection between vision and sight.

Acts 9:3. Some visions may be preceded by a bright light, as Saul experienced on the road to Damascus before his conversion after which his name was changed to Paul.

As he was traveling, it happened that he was approaching Damascus, and suddenly a light from heaven flashed around him;

Zechariah 4:2. What do you see, child of God? Exercise your vision for what you see is what you get.

He said to me, "What do you see?" And I said, "I see, and behold, a lampstand all of gold with its bowl on the top of it, and its seven lamps on it with seven spouts belonging to each of the lamps which are on the top of it;

Zechariah 5:2. Open your eyes to see.

And he said to me, "What do you see?" And I answered, "I see a flying scroll; its length is twenty cubits and its width ten cubits."

Zechariah 6:1.

Now I lifted up my eyes again and looked, and behold, four chariots were coming forth from between the two mountains; and the mountains were bronze mountains.

Visions, dreams and warnings

Matthew 2:12. God sometimes speaks to warns us.

And having been warned by God in a dream not to return to Herod, the magi left for their own country by another way.

Matthew 27:19.

While he was sitting on the judgment seat, his wife sent him a message, saying, "Have nothing to do with that righteous Man; for last night I suffered greatly in a dream because of Him."

Acts 22:18.

…and I saw Him saying to me, 'Make haste, and get out of Jerusalem quickly, because they will not accept your testimony about Me.'

Matthew 2:13. God spoke to Joseph in a dream to flee from Herod and save baby Jesus from death.

Now when they had gone, behold, an angel of the Lord appeared to Joseph in a dream and said, "Get up! Take the Child and His mother and flee to Egypt, and remain there until I tell you; for Herod is going to search for the Child to destroy Him."

Acts 16:9-10. God will sometimes confirm His mission and purpose for our lives through a vision.

And a vision appeared to Paul in the night. A man of Macedonia stood and pleaded with him, saying, "Come over to Macedonia and help us." Now after he had seen the vision, immediately we sought to go to Macedonia, concluding that the Lord had called us to preach the gospel to them.

Acts 18:9. God may use visions to encourage us.

Now the Lord spoke to Paul in the night by a vision, "Do not be afraid, but speak, and do not keep silent; for I am with you, and no one will attack you to hurt you; for I have many people in this city." And he continued there a year and six months, teaching the word of God among them.

Acts 27:23. God can also send angels in human form.

For this very night an angel of the God to whom I belong and whom I serve stood before me,

2 Corinthians 12:1-4. Paul's revelation and vision of Paradise

It is doubtless not profitable for me to boast. I will come to visions and revelations of the Lord I know a man in Christ who fourteen years ago—whether in the body I do not know, or whether out of the body I do not know, God knows—such a one was caught up to the third heaven. And I know such a man—whether in the body or out of the body I do not know, God knows— how he was caught up into Paradise and heard inexpressible words, which it is not lawful for a man to utter.

God may also communicate His purpose to different people who are not yet known to each other, as in the following two examples.

Acts 9:10-11. Ananias's vision.

Now there was a disciple at Damascus named Ananias; and the Lord said to him in a vision, "Ananias." And he said, "Here I am, Lord." And the Lord said to him, "Get up and go to the street called Straight, and inquire at the house of Judas for a man from Tarsus named Saul, for he is praying,

Acts 10:3. God communicates with a centurion named Cornelius in a dream.

About the ninth hour of the day he clearly saw in a vision an angel of God who had just come in and said to him, "Cornelius!"

Acts 10:9-11, 17. Peter's vision and instruction as God prepared him to meet with Cornelius.

The next day, as they went on their journey and drew near the city, Peter went up on the housetop to pray, about the sixth hour. Then he became very hungry and wanted to eat; but while they made ready, he fell into a trance and saw heaven opened and an object like a great sheet bound at the four corners, descending to him and let down to the earth. Now while Peter wondered within himself what this vision which he had seen meant, behold, the men who had been sent from Cornelius had made inquiry for Simon's house, and stood before the gate.

God also speaks to us in a clear voice.

Revelation 1:9-12. John's Vision of the Son of Man

I, John, both your brother and companion in the tribulation and kingdom and patience of Jesus Christ, was on the island that is called Patmos for the word of God and for the testimony of Jesus Christ. I was in the Spirit on the Lord's Day, and I heard behind me a loud voice, as of a trumpet, saying, "I am the Alpha and the Omega, the First and the Last," and, "What you see, write in a book and send it to the seven churches which are in Asia: to Ephesus, to Smyrna, to Pergamos, to Thyatira, to Sardis, to Philadelphia, and to Laodicea." Then I turned to see the voice that spoke with me. And having turned I saw seven golden lampstands.

Reflect:

How is God leading you in ministry and service as you read this book? Get a notebook and take notes. Remember to date your reflections.

In 3 months come back and appreciate what the LORD will have manifested in your life because of your obedient actions.

Chapter Eleven: **Five Victory Keys**

Life is a series of decisions. Our decision cause us to take certain actions which in turn lead to certain habits that shape our character and impart our destination.

The believer's decision must be wise and biblically based rather than based on emotions.

In this life everything starts with a decision. There is a difference between making a *quality* decision and deciding or planning. A *quality decision* is a choice that matches God's desire for your life, moving you forward from one step to another.

God called Moses as His prophet to lead His people out of captivity. Moses could have chosen to reject God's call, yet he decided to obey. God's miracles were manifested through Moses' obedience. Read Moses' encounter through the burning bush in Exodus 4:

> *Then Moses answered and said, "But suppose they will not believe me or listen to my voice; suppose they say, 'The Lord has not appeared to you.' " So the Lord said to him, **"What is that in your hand?" He said, "A rod."** And He said, "Cast it on the ground." So he cast it on the ground, and it became a serpent; and Moses fled from it.*

When the Lord said to Moses, "Reach out your hand and take it by the tail" (and he reached out his hand and caught it, and it became a rod in his hand), **"that they may believe that the Lord God of their fathers, the God of Abraham, the God of Isaac, and the God of Jacob, has appeared to you."**

Furthermore the Lord said to him, "Now put your hand in your bosom." And he put his hand in his bosom, and when he took it out, behold, his hand was leprous, like snow. And He said, "Put your hand in your bosom again." So he put his hand in his bosom again, and drew it out of his bosom, and behold, it was restored like his other flesh. "Then it will be, if they do not believe you, nor heed the message of the first sign, that they may believe the message of the latter sign. ...

Then Moses said to the Lord, "O my Lord, I am not eloquent, neither before nor since You have spoken to Your servant; but I am slow of speech and slow of tongue."

Moses made various excuses to try and get out of this assignment. Yet the LORD encouraged him and used what Moses had in his hand: the rod as a contact point for the numerous signs and wonders God would perform through him.

So the Lord said to him, "Who has made man's mouth? Or who makes the mute, the deaf, the seeing, or the blind? Have not I, the Lord? **Now therefore, go, and I will be with your mouth and teach you what you shall say."** *But he said, "O my Lord, please send by the hand of whomever else You may send."*

So the anger of the Lord was kindled against Moses, and He said: "Is not Aaron the Levite your brother? I know that he can speak well. And look, he is also coming out to meet you. **When he sees you, he will be glad in his heart. Now you shall speak to him and put the words in his mouth. And I will be with your mouth and with his mouth, and I will teach you what you shall do.** *So he shall be your spokesman to the people. And he himself shall be as a mouth for you, and you shall be to him as God.* **And you shall take this rod in your hand, with which you shall do the signs.**" (Emphasis mine)

When we hand over our concerns and deficiencies to the LORD, He provides able helpers to walk with us and encourage us along our journey of faith. God provided Aaron who was Moses' older brother to be his mouthpiece. However, God spoke directly to Moses who then relayed the message to Aaron.

Consider: Are you hesitant like Moses to heed God's instruction? Who has God called you to work with?

Key 1: Vision

What is vision and why do we need it in our spiritual lives? Without a vision you cannot stand even if you pray.

Consider: What is your vision? Have you fulfilled it or is it still in the works?

1 Corinthians 15:2 admonishes to "*hold fast that word which I preached to you...*" Verse 7 describes how the disciples' vision was illuminated after they met the risen Christ. *After that He was seen by James, then by all the apostles.*

Paul further describes his transformation from persecuting Christians after Jesus Christ revealed Himself, in verses 8-11.

> *Then last of all He was seen by me also, as by one born out of due time. For I am the least of the apostles, who am not worthy to be called an apostle, because I persecuted the church of God.* **But by the grace of God I am what I am, and His grace toward me was not in vain;** *but I labored more abundantly than they all, yet not I, but the grace of God which was with me. Therefore, whether it was I or they, so we preach and so you believed.* (Emphasis mine)

Who has spoken a word of encouragement into your life? Have you considered what motivated them to reach out to you with the Gospel of Jesus Christ? Thank God for inspiring them to touch your heart with God's love.

Reflect on the value of your vision. Your vision is tied to your destiny in God. Your vision should excite you to be the best version of you possible. You are who God says you are in Christ Jesus, therefore flow in what God has called you to.

The value of your vision pushes you to pray for your loved ones. Has someone abused or misused you? Continue to cry out to God for their salvation and redemption. As God saved and transformed Paul's life, He can do the same for your persecutors. The Spirit of the LORD will continually heal your wounded heart as you open up to Him. Our God is a consuming fire. He will consume every pain from your past that has kept you from following your God-given vision.

Whoever does not have a vision cannot become great. Whatever God proclaims about you will come to pass in due season, in Jesus' Matchless Name.

Hebrews 2:2 - *For if the word spoken through angels proved steadfast, and every transgression and disobedience received a just reward.*

Proverbs 29:18 – *Where there is no revelation, the people cast off restraint; but happy is he who keeps the law.*

You grow where there is a vision. Vision involves people. The vision must breathe life. Find ways to make your ministry enjoyable and fulfilling. Since the vision is for an appointed time, it is essential to wait patiently for it to be fulfilled. Pray according to your vision and walk towards it.

Psalm 42:5 reminds us that all we hold on to is our dream.

Prayer*: LORD, give me a good heart. All I desire is a pure and holy heart that pleases You.*

Each one of us has two types of people within us. One person wants to do good and follow God. The second person wants to follow the flesh and do whatever they desire without any regard for the consequences. We need to shake off the spirit of heaviness which the LORD says comes from our wounded heart.

God calls us to partake of Economic development wherever He has planted us so that we can serve Him joyfully where He sends us.

Declare:

Great things will be done to me as I obey the LORD and cooperate with the Holy Spirit in the mighty Name of Jesus.

I declare that in this season:

- I will be focused

- I will be diligent

- I will be single-minded

This year I will receive all my answers in Jesus' Mighty Name.

Amen.

Key 2: Prayer is our Power Weapon

Daniel 1:3 records, *Then the king instructed Ashpenaz, the master of his eunuchs, to bring some of the children of Israel and some of the king's descendants and some of the nobles...*

The king instructed his officials to choose some young men who had no blemish, were good looking and gifted in all wisdom. He dressed them for leadership.

Read Daniel's Prayer in chapter 9:9. To the Lord our God belong mercy and forgiveness, even when we rebel. When Daniel was told that he could no longer pray to God for 30 days, to comply with the king's ruling, he refused and continued praying to his God. After he was thrown into the den of hungry lions, God shut the lions' mouths and saved Daniel's life. The astonished king then made a ruling that the whole land must honour and worship the God Daniel prayed to.

In another incident Daniel was tested for 21 days. God revealed the dream to him. In Daniel 3:13 God saved the three young men Shadrack, Meshack and Abednego from the fiery furnace. Daniel was promoted to serve before the king's palace.

After Joseph had spent two years in prison after he was falsely accused by Potiphar's wife, he was elevated to second in command to Potiphar. God chooses people who can take care of His property. Example, faith and courage in God.

Your good looks don't come from the food you eat, it comes from your dedication to God.

..Daniel 9 - Daniel's Prayer for the People

In the first year of Darius the son of Ahasuerus, of the lineage of the Medes, who was made king over the realm of the Chaldeans— in the first year of his reign I, Daniel, understood by the books the number of the years specified by the word of the Lord through Jeremiah the prophet, that He would accomplish seventy years in the desolations of Jerusalem. **Then I set my face toward the Lord God to make request by prayer and supplications, with fasting, sackcloth, and ashes.** (Emphasis mine)

When God instructs you to pray, pray like Daniel did. God showed him that Jerusalem's desolation would last for 70 years from the first year of Darius' reign of the Babylonian kingdom. Daniel understood the interpretation of the word given to Jeremiah the prophet and was quick to respond by interceding for the land. He pleaded with God in prayer, petition, fasting, sackcloth and ashes (v1-3).

For 70 years God was not present in the land. The devil set out to mindlessly torture the inhabitants with all forms of sickness. This is also evident in the times we are living in. Daniel stood in the gap, took the transgressions of the Babylonians and the children of Israel. He confessed the sins the people had committed as though he was the one who had wronged God (v4-9).

And I prayed to the Lord my God, and made confession, and said, "O Lord, great and awesome God, who keeps His covenant and mercy with those who love Him, and with those who keep His commandments, we have sinned and committed iniquity, we have done wickedly and rebelled, even by departing from Your precepts and Your judgments. Neither have we heeded Your servants the prophets, who spoke in Your name to our kings and our princes, to our fathers and all the people of the land. **O Lord, righteousness belongs to You,** but to us shame of face, as it is this day—to the men of Judah, to the inhabitants of Jerusalem and all Israel, those near and those far off in all the countries to which You have driven them, because of the unfaithfulness which they have committed against You. "O Lord, to us belongs shame of face, to our kings, our princes, and our fathers, because we have sinned against You. **To the Lord our God belong mercy and forgiveness, though we have rebelled against Him.** (Emphasis mine)

Daniel, understanding the implications of the people's sin against God, pleaded fervently for God to show them mercy, forgive and help them turn their eyes back to Him. Further in verses 10-12, Daniel recounted the wondrous deliverance God had performed for the people in Moses' time.

We have not obeyed the voice of the Lord our God, to walk in His laws, which He set before us by His servants the prophets… "As it is written in the Law of Moses, all this disaster has come upon us; yet we have not made our prayer before the Lord our God, that we might turn from our iniquities and understand Your truth. **Therefore the Lord has kept the disaster in mind, and brought it upon us; for the Lord our God is righteous in all the works which He does, though we have not obeyed His voice.** *And now, O Lord our God, who brought Your people out of the land of Egypt with a mighty hand, and made Yourself a name, as it is this day—we have sinned, we have done wickedly!*

God's righteousness is never in question. He is abiding in lovingkindness and tender mercies. However, our just God will not condone wickedness among His children.

Daniel's prayer for mercy over God's chosen people demonstrate his total commitment, calling and service to God's children (v16-19).

"O Lord, according to all Your righteousness, I pray, let Your anger and Your fury be turned away from Your city Jerusalem, Your holy mountain; because for our sins, and for the iniquities of our fathers, Jerusalem and Your people are a reproach to all those around us.

Now therefore, our God, hear the prayer of Your servant, and his supplications, and for the Lord's sake cause Your face to shine on Your sanctuary, which is desolate. O my God, incline Your ear and hear; open Your eyes and see our desolations, and the city which is called by Your name; for we do not present our supplications before You because of our righteous deeds, but because of Your great mercies. O Lord, hear! O Lord, forgive! O Lord, listen and act! Do not delay for Your own sake, my God, for Your city and Your people are called by Your name." (Emphasis mine)

May God shine His face upon His people and His sanctuary and incline His ear to our cry when we are in distress. Whenever you are in distress commit this prayer before the LORD in total faith. May God deliver you and grant you His unfailing mercy through every storm in Jesus' Mighty Name.

Key 3: God's Guiding Word

As we live in these uncertain days let us focus on LORD who is our Alpha and the Omega. John 15 :1-4 declares,

> *"I am the true vine, and My Father is the vinedresser. Every branch in Me that does not bear fruit He takes away; and every branch that bears fruit He prunes, that it may bear more fruit. You are already clean because of the word which I have spoken to you. Abide in Me, and I in you. As the branch cannot bear fruit of itself, unless it abides in the vine, neither can you, unless you abide in Me.*

The Bible illustrates that our Father is the true Gardener. He cuts off every branch in us that bears no fruit and prunes every branch that bears fruit, to increase its fruitfulness. Whatever produces fruit is pruned so that it bears an abundance of new fruit.

God's pruning cleans His children. Jesus urged us to remain in Him as He dwells in us because we cannot bear fruit on our own. Our fruit can only be nourished when we remain in God the Father and the Holy Spirit.

Choose to daily remain in Him so that you will bear much fruit. Remaining Him also involves dwelling on His Word. We are assured that God will grant us whatever we desire and ask for in His will. Without the Father we can do nothing (v5), yet in Him we live and move and have our being. (Acts 17:28)

The key to *receiving* God's blessings lies in the *asking*, as John 15:7 reveals; *If you abide in Me, and My words abide in you, you will ask what you desire, and it shall be done for you.*

God is calling us to a joyful life of wisdom, worship and grace as we dwell on His Living Word (Colossians 3:16). The New International Version refers to songs of the Spirit:

> *Let the message (Word) of Christ dwell among you richly as you teach and admonish one another with all wisdom through psalms, hymns, and songs from the Spirit, singing to God with gratitude in your hearts."*

The Holy Spirit reveals God's glory as He ministers to us, creating a bubbling over of joyful praise, worship and thanksgiving. Dwelling in close connection with the LORD grows our spiritual connection and deepens our relationship to the Father.

God also protects us through His Word (Ephesians 6:17): *And take the helmet of salvation, and the sword of the Spirit, which is the word of God.*

God's Word lights our path, helping us to tread safely through life's unexpected moments (Psalm 119:105): *Your word is a lamp for my feet, a light on my path.*

When you are totally immersed in the Word of God, you are full of God Himself. God is His Word. When you apply the helmet of salvation and the sword of the Spirit of God, you are empowered, fully loaded to stand and fight the enemy.

God's Word empowers His children through His Word.

> *For the word of God is living and powerful, and sharper than any two-edged sword, piercing even to the division of soul and spirit, and of joints and marrow, and is a discerner of the thoughts and intents of the heart. (Hebrews 4:12)*

God examines our hearts, while man focuses on outward appearance. The LORD revealed this profound truth to the prophet Samuel when he went to anoint a king for the children of Israel. While Samuel looked at Jesse's strong looking sons, thinking, *"Could this be the one?"* God refocused Samuel's heart to use spiritual insight, as 1 Samuel 16:7 reveals,

> *But the Lord said to Samuel, "Do not look at his appearance or at his physical stature, because I have refused (rejected) him. For the Lord does not see as man sees; for man looks at the outward appearance, but the Lord looks at the heart."*

Isaiah 55:11 guides us on how to declare the Word of God so that we will receive our blessing as we remain in total faith.

> *So shall My word be that goes forth from My mouth; it shall not return to Me void, but it shall accomplish what I please, and it shall prosper in the thing for which I sent it.*

Once you stand on the Word of God, you can command anything, and it will be accomplished. John 1:1 declares, *In the beginning was the Word, and the Word was with God, and the Word was God.* God's Word which has always existed from the beginning is still alive and active today. Apply the Word to unlock your doors of breakthrough.

Therefore, be careful what you speak as it will come to pass. Do not joke about the things of God when you are full of the Spirit God. Speak only what is worthy by guarding your tongue. Heed the Word in 2 Timothy 3:16-17 which equips us for service in the LORD's Vineyard.

> *All Scripture is given by inspiration of God, and is profitable for doctrine, for reproof, for correction, for instruction in righteousness, that the man of God may be complete, thoroughly equipped for every good work.*

Apply the spiritual wisdom apostle Paul revealed in Philippians 4:8-9 as you meditate on the Word:

> *Finally, brethren, whatever things are true, whatever things are noble, whatever things are just, whatever things are pure, whatever things are lovely, whatever things are of good report, if there is any virtue and if there is anything praiseworthy—meditate on these things. The things which you learned and received and heard and saw in me, these do, and the God of peace will be with you.*

Key 4: The Secret of Love

1 Corinthians 13: The Greatest Gift

Though I speak with the tongues of men and of angels, but have not love, I have become sounding brass or a clanging cymbal. And though I have the gift of prophecy, and understand all mysteries and all knowledge, and though I have all faith, so that I could remove mountains, but have not love, I am nothing. And though I bestow all my goods to feed the poor, and though I give my body to be burned, but have not love, it profits me nothing. Love suffers long and is kind; love does not envy; love does not parade itself, is not puffed up; does not behave rudely, does not seek its own, is not provoked, [thinks no evil; does not rejoice in iniquity, but rejoices in the truth; bears all things, believes all things, hopes all things, endures all things. Love never fails. But whether there are prophecies, they will fail; whether there are tongues, they will cease; whether there is knowledge, it will vanish away. For we know in part and we prophesy in part. But when that which is perfect has come, then that which is in part will be done away. When I was a child, I spoke as a child, I understood as a child, I thought as a child; but when I became a man, I put away childish things.

For now we see in a mirror, dimly, but then face to face. Now I know in part, but then I shall know just as I also am known. And now abide faith, hope, love, these three; but the greatest of these is love.

Pray for understanding of how to apply the principle of LOVE revealed in 1 Corinthians 13.

Psalm 119:130 says, *The entrance of Your word gives light.* Let us reflect on the characteristics of LOVE, as revealed in verses 4-7.

Love is patient. Are you patient?

Love is kind. Are you kind?

It does not envy or boast. Are you boastful?

Do you look down on people who don't have?

Do you dishonour others and get away with it?

It is not self-seeking or easily angered.

Do you get angry or fume when someone mistreats you?

Love keeps no record of wrong. This is a biggie.

A word of caution to married men and women: remembering the wrongs your spouse did to you does not demonstrate love.

If you have all this resentment in yourself, check yourself and ask God to help you to release and forgive those who have wronged you.

If I regard iniquity in my heart the LORD will not hear. (Psalm 66:18)

Personal testimony:

As a child growing up my dad used to love me dearly. His love was extreme. For example, Dad often told my mother, "*If you wake up one morning and decide to give away our children, you can't give Harriet away. She is mine.*"

He would give me anything I requested of him. However, despite all the immense love Dad had for me, he could not fill the emptiness in my heart until I received the love of God in my heart.

That was when I felt that I had everything I wanted in this world. If Mom was late to prepare my morning tea, Dad would take me to a restaurant and buy me breakfast before dropping me off at school.

The same is true for many around the world. Many people are busy working hard to buy material things like posh cars, houses and more. However, these material things cannot fill the vacuum in the heart which can only be filled by the love of God.

People even take drugs to feel loved. When we experience and embrace the love of God, we have everything.

Key 5. Obedience to God's Call

Obedience is an essential ingredient to walking successfully with God. Read God's Commission to Joshua, recorded in Joshua 1:

> *After the death of Moses the servant of the Lord, it came to pass that the Lord spoke to Joshua the son of Nun, Moses' assistant, saying: "Moses My servant is dead. Now therefore, arise, go over this Jordan, you and all this people, to the land which I am giving to them—the children of Israel. **Every place that the sole of your foot will tread upon I have given you, as I said to Moses.** From the wilderness and this Lebanon as far as the great river, the River Euphrates, all the land of the Hittites, and to the Great Sea toward the going down of the sun, shall be your territory. No man shall be able to stand before you all the days of your life; as I was with Moses, so I will be with you. I will not leave you nor forsake you. **Be strong and of good courage, for to this people you shall divide as an inheritance the land which I swore to their fathers to give them**. Only be strong and very courageous, that you may observe to do according to all the law which Moses My servant commanded you; do not turn from it to the right hand or to the left, that you may prosper wherever you go.* (Emphasis mine)

Why did God repeat the words, **Be strong and courageous**? He must have known that Joshua would need inner strength to fulfil God's call upon his life. Joshua needed to consistently look upwards for renewal, restoration and resourcing spiritually and emotionally. Meditating on the Word was a prerequisite for a lasting relationship with his Heavenly Father and Guide (v8-9).

> *This Book of the Law shall not depart from your mouth, but you shall meditate in it day and night, that you may observe to do according to all that is written in it.* *For then you will make your way prosperous, and then you will have good success. Have I not commanded you?* ***Be strong and of good courage; do not be afraid, nor be dismayed, for the Lord your God is with you wherever you go.***" (Emphasis mine)

Whenever God instructs us to be bold and courageous, it is because He is preparing us for a sensitive mission that requires daily grace. He instructed Joshua to guide the children of Israel to the Promised Land after Moses died, since Joshua had a good track record of obedience, faith and dependability. Joshua had faithfully served under Moses in the ministry. Now that his leader had departed to glory, Joshua needed to step up and complete the task Moses started.

Emboldened, Joshua confidently guided the children of Israel on what they should do to possess their inheritance (v10-13). A certain order was to be followed by every tribe.

Then Joshua commanded the officers of the people, saying, **"Pass through the camp and command the people, saying, 'Prepare provisions for yourselves, for within three days you will cross over this Jordan, to go in to possess the land which the Lord your God is giving you to possess.' "** *And to the Reubenites, the Gadites, and half the tribe of Manasseh...* **"Remember the word which Moses the servant of the Lord commanded you, saying, 'The Lord your God is giving you rest and is giving you this land.'** (Emphasis mine)

Notice how the people pledged their new allegiance to Joshua (v16-18), ending with the familiar encouragement, *Only be strong and of good courage.*

God instructs us when we obey Him. Moses is like our old nature which is gone when we meet with the LORD. We each enter this world at one stop and exit at another. Meanwhile, God's mission on earth will invariably be accomplished. That is why He passes the baton to the next person identified for the task. He trains us in righteousness so that we can effectively serve in His Vineyard.

REFLECTIONS

Moses is no more, but God is continuing His work and purpose for our lives.

Sometimes we give up on our dreams when we lose our loved ones. God's promise remains true, therefore carry on with your dream. Your territory will extend from the Great River, …

No one will be able to stand against you all the days of your life.

What is making you fearful?

Why are you failing? God has promised no one will stand against you all the days of your life…

You and I are the Moses and Joshua of today. We need to carry on the work they started and fulfil our God given purse on Earth.

Pastor Morris Cerrulo, Evangelists Reinhart Bonnke and Billy Graham are no more, but God will never leave us nor forsake us. No matter how hard the situation is, God is right there.

Be strong and courageous. You will lead these people to inherit the land. Sometimes we feel like giving up. God repeated the words to Joshua: *Be strong and courageous.*

Do not turn to the left or to the right. May you be successful wherever you go.

Reflect on Joshua 1:9-10, *Do not let this Book of the Law depart from your mouth...Do everything written in it... THEN you will be prosperous and successful. Have I not commanded you? Be strong and courageous. Do not be terrified, nor discouraged, for the LORD will be with you wherever you go.*

Serving God is a journey, therefore obey and trust God through your life's calling and ministry service. After Moses died, God did not stop there. He continued with the work He had begun. Be encouraged to continue in what God has called you to. Be strong and you will inherit your promised possession.

No man will be able to stand against you all your days on earth.

Now my old nature is dead, therefore I must take people to inherit the land. Wherever I am belongs to God.

I am leading these people to posses the land. Whatever the devil has taken away, I am standing to take possession of what belongs to us with God's help.

Be careful to obey all the Law My servant Moses gave you.

We will only be successful through our obedience. It is not from working hard. Let us be careful not to leave the place and calling God has given us. When we leave His path, we fight enemies without any back up. On the other hand, every time we obey, we are successful and blessed.

Meditate upon this Book of the Law day and night...

Reflect on God's Word, weigh the Word, apply the Word in every area of your life.

Those who know and obey God's Word will be prosperous and successful. They will live righteously and achieve God's purpose and goals for their lives.

Requirements for a prosperous and successful life:

- Obey God's Word and Law
- Be strong, courageous and diligent
- Meditate on God's Word
- Make God's Word your authoritative guide for every plan and action
- Daily study and meditate on God's Word
- Earnestly seek God's presence throughout your life

If you do all this, you will live a successful life.

However, we must never conclude that God is bound to furnish material prosperity to everyone who follows these conditions.

Such general principles are not absolute guarantees, for they are subject to God's higher choices for each of us.

Sometimes God permits us to undergo much pain and suffering so that we may seek His face and live successfully. Joshua is dead. Identify yourself to God and be yourself for service of God.

In Joshua 1:3 – *I have given you every place your feet tread*. This means even in challenging nations, God has given you that land as your inheritance.

If people say it is impossible, God says it is POSSIBLE. Just make up your mind and go for it. You are called to do something so that you may live a prosperous and successful life.

Conclusion

As you consider your life's purpose and calling, write down your vision for how you put the tips shared in this book into practice.

Ask God to guide you and lead you to those who He has reserved to help you accomplish your work on earth.

Finally, *what has most inspired you from my journey?*

What resonated with your own journey?

What nugget are you grateful for unlocking today?

How will you move forward, ensuing you stay on track with serving the ministry gifts God has already deposited into your life and spirit?

Write your vision, make it plain.

Then action what you desire as you prayerfully step into your next level of service with a joyful heart.

I appreciate you for taking the time to read this book. Share your testimony and one breakthrough on Instagram at:

https://www.instagram.com/harrietanderson1045/

About the Author

Bishop Harriet Ssempala Anderson is an entrepreneur and coach called as a mother to many nations. She is the proverbial woman with a coat of many colours favoured by God. *The coat of many colours* represents the royalty and favour received when one joins God's family as a born-again Christian.

Based in the United Kingdom, the author has travelled globally preaching the gospel of the Lord Jesus, reaching the lost for Christ. A self-taught fashion designer, her passion is designing individuals after God's heart physically and spiritually to enrich and transform lives.

Bishop Harriet and her husband Pastor Simon Anderson jointly serve in Abundance Ministries.

Connect with the author:

https://www.abundanceministries.co.uk/

IG: https://www.instagram.com/harrietanderson1045/

For other books by the author visit:

https://www.amazon.co.uk/Bishop-Harriet-S-Anderson/e/B0BLP8TQGB/

Check out the Author's books:

https://www.amazon.co.uk/Bishop-Harriet-S-Anderson/e/B0BLP8TQGB/

Praying God's Word

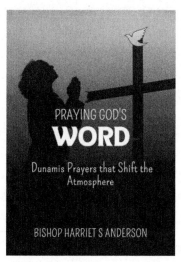

A Closer Walk with God

Great Awakening book series